GRAPHIC DESIGNERS TOOLBOX:

A resource for aspiring or new graphic designers with 3 years experience and under.

By: NaTasha Ashton, BFA

Copyright © 2023 NaTasha Ashton

All rights reserved. No part of this book may be reproduced in any form on by an electronic or mechanical means, including information storage and retrieval systems, without permission in writing from the publisher, except by a reviewer who may quote brief passages in a review.

Printed in the United States of America

ISBN: 978-1-329-53226-7

Lulu Press, Inc.

www.lulu.com

Design and publishing by:

Ashton Creative Group, LLC.

Harvest Publishing Group, LLC.

CONTENTS

Acknowledgments

Dedication

Chapter 1: The Beginnings

Chapter 2: Graphic Design 101

Chapter 3: Typography

Chapter 4: Color Theory

Chapter 5: Vector vs Raster

Chapter 6: The importance of contracts

Chapter 7: Elements and Principles of Art

Chapter 8: Find your Flow

Chapter 9: The Software: its purpose

Chapter 10: Negative Space

ACKNOWLEDGEMENTS

- I want to thank my Lord and Savior Jesus Christ for blessing me with the gift and ability to write. I give you all glory! I do not take this gift and anointing lightly.
- I want to thank my husband, Paul E. Ashton. Thank you babe for your support and encouragement during this process. I love you so much sweetheart!
- I want to thank my Alma Mater, Virginia State University for help me the gain the tools, knowledge as a graphic designer.

DEDICATION

I want to dedicate this book to my mother Cecelia Ann Merritt Heath. Words can't express how much I miss you and appreciate you. Thank you mommy for seeing something in me to pursue art and design! You are a precious jewel. Thank you for your love and support. You were and still are an awesome mommy. Hugs and kisses forever.

December 19, 1954 - April 21, 2013

Love your baby girl,

Tasha

CHAPTER 1

The Beginning: How it started!

As a child, I developed a love for painting, coloring, arts & crafts and so on. I stated playing around with graphic design as a young adult. Then I decided to make this her career.

I got serious about graphic design when I enrolled at Virginia State University as a Visual Communications major in August 2006. In May 2010, I graduated from Virginia State University with a Bachelors in Fine Arts in Visual Communications (Graphic Design).From there I continued to perfect my craft and continued as a business owner/entrepreneur.

Here is a rundown of my testimony:
•Doctors gave me and my mom up.
•Both having a 40/40 chance of survival
•I was born by C-Section
•On oxygen for 6 months
•In an incubator 6 months
•Because of the oxygen and the fact I was a micro preemie I weighted LESS then a pound my eyes didn't develop.
•I have NO sight in my left eye
•I have Glaucoma, Astigmatism, and cataracts in my right eye.
•Tube scars on my hands be chest.
____-

- I had a MAJOR STROKE while being 9 weeks pregnant in 2019
- I sat in pool of my own blood (Hematoma) in April of 2020 after having my baby boy in March 2020. I had to get 3 blood transfusions.
- I had 85 pounds of fluid in my body for over a year in 2021.

I say all of that to encourage you to let you know YOU CAN DO IT. Being the graphic design industry is hard, a lot of competition but God will give you everything you need. A lot of people ask me how I do what I do being visually impaired and legally blind. My response is IT'S ALL GOD! My desire to break barriers and overcome all odds. Be encouraged!

CHAPTER 2
Graphic Design 101

What is graphic design? Graphic Design is communicating visually though images, photography, and typography.

According to AIGA, graphic design is also known as communication design, is the art and practice of planning and projecting ideas and experiences with visual and textual content. The form of the communication can be physical or virtual, and may include images, words, or graphic forms. The experience can take place in an instant or over a long period of time. The work can happen at any scale, from the design of a single postage stamp to a national postal signage system, or from a company's digital avatar to the sprawling and interlinked digital and physical content of an international newspaper. It can also be for any purpose, whether commercial, educational, cultural, or political.

What do Graphic Designers Do?

A graphic designer is visual storyteller. Our job is to blend text, color, images into a composition that gives a message. So we communicate visually.

What skills does a Graphic Designer need?

- Knowledge of Adobe Creative Cloud
- Sketching/drawing

- Creativity
- Deadline Oriented - Meeting deadlines is very, very important.
- Sketching/Drawing (optional)
- Attention to detail
- *and more.*

The different types of Graphic Designers

There are several different types of graphic designers. Here are the most common types:

- **Branding Specialists:** A branding specialist is a graphic designer who specializes in creating visuals for branding purposes. This might include developing logos, crafting marketing materials, and creating overall brand guidelines.
- **Marketing Designers:** A marketing designer creates visuals for use in marketing and advertising campaigns. This could involve designing website banners, crafting email newsletters, or developing print ads.
- **Packaging Designers:** Packaging designers are responsible for the design of product packaging, such as boxes, bottles, and labels. In some cases, they may also be involved in the design of retail displays.
- **User Interface Designers:** User interface (UI) designers create interfaces for digital products, such as websites and mobile apps. Their goal is to create an intuitive and user-friendly experience for users.

- **Motion Graphic Designers:** Motion graphics are a type of graphic design that uses animation and video to create visually stimulating content. Motion graphics designers use a variety of software programs to create their work, such as After Effects and Maya.
- **Animation Designers:** Animation is a type of motion graphic that brings static images to life. Animators use various techniques to animate their designs, such as stop-motion and traditional hand-drawn animation.
- **Game Designers:** Game designers are responsible for the visual elements of video games. This includes creating the game's characters, scenery, and user interface. In some cases, they may also be involved in the game's development process.
- **Illustrators:** Illustrators use their artistic talent to create a variety of visuals, such as book covers, company logos, and product packaging. While they may use software programs to help with the creation process, their work is largely hand-drawn.

What Graphic Design is NOT

Graphic Design is not Photoshop, Illustrator, InDesign, Muse, Dreamweaver, or any program within the Creative Cloud. Those are simply tools. The creation comes from the **MIND** and **HAND** of the designer. Remember our job is NOT to make things pretty, but our job is to make things FUNCTIONAL. We are problem solvers. I believe making pretty design s is a by product of a well designed functional piece.

What is Branding?

Before I go any further, your logo is NOT your brand. Branding is the marketing practice of creating a name, symbol or design that identifies and differentiates a product from other products. From additional study, I learned 10 myths of what graphic design

Myth#1 Graphic design is all about branding

It's common that a logo is the face of any brand that is designed for the target audience to interact with the brand through it. So it is definitely important that a professional graphic designer produces logos and is keen on branding.

Myth#2 Graphic design is all about fonts

The art of text layout is one of the key elements for creating a beautiful design. However, it's not just about choosing a font that looks good. You have to think about what type of font is right
to **communicate your brand**, values, and target audience, but typography isn't the only thing to consider when it comes to graphic design.
It's all about the interaction between text and other elements on the page, including images, graphics, shapes, lines, borders, and white space. To create a powerful design, they all need to work together in perfect synchronicity.

Myth#3 Graphics is for printed media only

So wrong! In the last decades, the world has been almost completely digitalized, the application of graphic design, in fact, is used more on digital platforms than on print media.

Website design, social media design, **video design**, email design, and more are just a few examples that can clearly debunk this graphic design myth. Whether it's YouTube channel design, email headers, Facebook covers, or blog banners, every web or social media platform uses different graphic designs.

Myth#4 Graphic design has nothing to do with motions

Graphic design is no longer limited to regular images or graphics. And video continues to emerge as one of the **most powerful advertising media** out there.

Animation and video are becoming an important part of the **graphic design toolbox**. This includes GIFs, graphics for YouTube videos, animated infographics, and social media ads with slideshows of images and graphics, etc.

Myth#5 Graphic design is all about creating 100% original designs

Uniqueness is important. It makes your brand stand out from the crowd and outrun the competitors. However, this does not mean that there's a need to create **designs from scratch** each time you need typical visuals.

Even professional graphic designers create multiple templates to optimize the processes in case they have to create similar assets on a regular basis. It allows them to achieve consistency across all brand materials. That's normal to use samples.

Myth#6 You don't need to budget
In fact, this is one of the most misleading graphic design myths. Since graphic design, today has become an essential part of effective branding and marketing for any business, large or small, only experienced designers may understand the nuances and importance of using properly designed graphics. And this is already about the budget as they should be paid up.

Moreover, visuals today play a key role in creating a name for a brand and determine the success of a company, both on and off the digital platform. This is why it is also so important to create a graphic design budget for your business.

Myth#7 Graphic design is all about beautiful designs

One of the biggest common misconceptions about graphic design is that it simply makes things beautiful or aesthetically pleasing. However, this is not always the case.

The beauty of the design is essentially a pillar that helps grab the attention of potential customers. Sometimes it shocks the viewer, makes them emotion, makes them think, or even makes them react & interact, etc.

Myth#8 Graphic design is all about following visual trends

Just like in product design, or any other creative industry, the trends in graphic design come and go quickly. In 2021, it was all about handwritten fonts, pastel colors, and textures or whiteboards. It's more likely that 2022 will bring a new crop of visuals. The job of graphic designers is to stay conscious but not become the slaves of changeable trends—all good what ends good.

Myth#9 You need to be talented to do graphic design

It's common that the majority of graphic designers are people with a nice taste, and visual flair, which is why they gravitate towards this field. However, you don't have to be a born creator to make up effective designs. Like any other activity, graphic design is a skill that can be mastered.

It's not just about feeling or seeing something unique and magically bringing it to life. Graphic design is not only about art but about science. There is a method and technique for this that begins with an awareness of the various elements that make up a powerful and effective design. Talent is not a guarantee and you have to learn a lot to polish your skills.

Myth#10 Graphic designers know everything

The truth is that they are not prophets of your brand vision or business goals. It must be understood that for a design project to be successful, there must be utmost clarity between the designer and the client.
It is essential that you, as a client, be clear about your vision and expectations from collaboration. Providing a detailed brief and communication from both sides will provide a common vision of the concept, eliminate misunderstandings and increase chances for success with minimum iterations.

Along with these graphic severe design myths, some myths are just ridiculous but also need to be destroyed. These may include (but are not limited to): Graphic design being very EASY, Graphic design making your business strive and really fast, editing and fixing the design being a snap, or calling anyone with basic Photoshop skills or similar – a professional designer, etc.

CHAPTER 3
Typography

Typography is EVERYWHERE! Signs, billboards, catalogs, and so much more. The fonts you use is very important because it can make or break your design.

Typography is the strategic arrangement of type in order to make written language readable and visually appealing. The art of typography is one of the most important skills every graphic and web designer needs to master. It's central to every form of design, both print and digital.

Typeface vs. font

The terms "typeface" and "font" are often used interchangeably. In fact, when most people say "font," what they're really referring to is a typeface. As a graphic designer, it's important to understand the difference between these terms.

A typeface is a family of fonts. Some familiar examples include Times New Roman, Arial, and Brush Script. A font is a variation of a typeface, typically bold, italic, or a combination of the two. Examples of fonts include Times New Roman Italic and Arial Bold.

Serif and San Serif

A Serif is a decorative line that is added to some letters at the beginning or/and at the end.

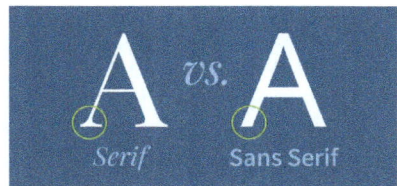

(*Image is from google.com*)

Three types of Serif fonts

There are three different kinds of serif typefaces: humanist, transitional, and slab serif. There are also a few more categories of serif typefaces, like Renaissance, baroque, modern, and wedge, but we'll focus on the three listed previously.

1. Humanist Serif

Humanist serif typefaces emulate classical calligraphy with contrasting strokes. Humanist typefaces were the first Roman typefaces. Other characteristics of Humanist typefaces are small x-height and low contrast between strokes. You'll often see classic and traditional content printed with a humanist serif typeface, like books and articles.

2. Transitional Serif

Transitional serif typefaces have sharper serifs and more contrasting strokes to create a style that's strong and dynamic, and is often used in law or academics. The influence of a pen is gone with Transitional typefaces. An example of this is through the vertical stress in the bowls of letters, meaning the thinnest part of the letter.

In a Transitional typeface the thinnest part is completely vertical, whereas in the Humanist typefaces, the vertical stress is actually on a diagonal, since that's how the vertical stress of a letter generally is when words are handwritten. Georgia and Baskerville are Transitional serif typefaces.

3. Slab serif

Slab Serif, or Egyptian or square serif, typefaces have heavy and boxy serifs with almost no contrast in the strokes of the letter. This creates a friendly yet authoritative feel, like in a marketing application. New typefaces were needed for advertising and such, so a bolder typeface was needed. Monospaced text is often considered to be Slab Serif. Popular Slab serif typefaces include Courier and Rockwell.

What is a Sans Serif font?

Sans serif typefaces are considered more modern than serif typefaces. They lack the strokes that distinguish a serif typeface, hence the use of the French word "sans," which means "without." Sans serif typefaces are often used to signify something clean, minimal, friendly, or modern.

Some of the most popular sans serif typefaces are Arial, Helvetica, Open Sans, Calibri, and Verdana. Pluralsight's official font (as seen in this post) is a Sans Serif font. Sans serif fonts are often used on the web for large groups of text because of the lower DPI (dots per inch) that screens have compared to print. They are also generally easier for children to read because they're simpler.

Why Typography is important?

1. Deliver a message

Graphic design is all about visual communication. Through typography, we can heighten the message of a design in a clear and legible way.

2. Create hierarchy

One important way typography is used in graphic design is to create visual hierarchy. This is often accomplished through sizing--the largest element on the page naturally draws the eye first. In a text-heavy graphic design, such as a newspaper or brochure, the headlines stand out and draw attention because they're larger than the body text.

Another way to create typographic hierarchy is through the combination of different typefaces.The standard approach is to establish three levels of typographic hierarchy: headings, subheadings, and body copy. Each level utilizes a different font, and the hierarchy is further established through sizing.

3. Build brand recognition

A powerful role of typography in graphic design is to establish and grow brand recognition. This is especially true when it comes to logo design. When you think about popular brands like Coca-Cola, Harley-Davidson, and Disney, you can easily visualize their unique logotype in your mind.

Creating brand recognition through typography helps create a unique attachment and feeling of familia.

4. Show personality

Some typefaces, particularly in the display category, add personality to a graphic design. The intentional use of typography can indicate whether a brand is playful, warm, mysterious, edgy, youthful, refined, and so on. Therefore, it's important to understand the traits of a brand or design project in order to use typography that conveys the right personality.

Bold and rounded typography is typically used to convey playfulness and friendliness in graphic design. In contrast, thin and subtle letterforms give off an air of sophistication and sincerity. With a little bit of practice, it's fairly easy to read the personality of a given typeface and decide whether it's a good fit for your project.

5. Make an impact

Typography can create a strong visual impact. There are many ways to get creative with typography in graphic design in order to make an impression on the viewer. It can even be used in such a way that no other supporting visuals are needed in order to effectively communicate the message of the design.

6. Establish a mood and tone

Similarly to how typography conveys personality, it also helps establish the mood and tone of a graphic design piece. In this way, typography visually brings out a brand's values, without needing to explicitly state what those values are. For instance, a brand that values minimalism can help convey this value through the use of a modern, lightweight sans serif font.Typography can also heighten the emotional factor of a piece of tex

7. Draw attention

One of the most important roles of typography is to draw attention to important messages. Typography is an easy and impactful method for making a word or phrase stand out in a design. Some ways to draw attention through typography include increasing the size, changing the color, and changing the font or typeface to contrast with the surrounding elements.

8. Create harmony and consistency

Typography helps create harmony and consistency in a design. In brand identity design, it's important to create visual consistency across all platforms. In website design, this looks like using consistent heading and body fonts throughout the site. Visual consistency creates a professional and streamlined look and promotes brand recognition. Harmony in graphic design refers to visual balance and continuity. Harmonious designs are easy to follow and aesthetically appealing.

Chapter 4

Color Theory

Color in design is just as important as typography. What is color theory? Color theory is the collection of rules and guidelines which designers use to communicate with users through appealing color schemes in visual interfaces.

There are three basic categories of color theory that are logical and useful : The color wheel, color harmony, and the context of how colors are used.

The Color Wheel

A color circle, based on red, yellow and blue, is traditional in the field of art. How was this developed? Sir Isaac Newton developed the first circular diagram of colors in 1666. Since then, scientists and artists have studied and designed numerous variations of this concept. Diagram is from google.

Primary Colors: Red, yellow and blue
In traditional color theory (used in paint and pigments), primary colors are the 3 pigment colors that cannot be mixed or formed by any combination of other colors. All other colors are derived from these 3 hues.

Secondary Colors: Green, orange and purple
These are the colors formed by mixing the primary colors.

Tertiary Colors: Yellow-orange, red-orange, red-purple, blue-purple, blue-green & yellow-green
These are the colors formed by mixing a primary and a secondary color. That's why the hue is a two word name, such as blue-green, red-violet, and yellow-orange.

Color Harmony

Harmony can be defined as a pleasing arrangement of parts, whether it be music, poetry, color, or even an ice cream sundae.

In visual experiences, harmony is something that is pleasing to the eye. It engages the viewer and it creates an inner sense of order, a balance in the visual experience.

8 Color Schemes

- **Complementary:** Complementary or opposite colors from the color wheel

- **Split Complementary:** Three colors—the main color and colors from either side of its complement

- **Triad:** Three colors from equidistant points on the color wheel

- **Monochromatic:** Different shades and depths of a single color

- **Analogous:** The main color and the colors from either side of it on the color wheel

- **Neutral:** Uses a color that has been reduced by adding black

- **Achromatic:** No color—just blacks, whites and greys

- **Secondary:** Green, purple and orange used together

Here are some of the most popular basic color schemes.

Complementary Color Schemes

The complementary scheme uses colors that are directly across from each other on the color wheel. Examples include:

- Red and Green
- Red-Orange and Blue-Green
- Orange and Blue
- Violet and Yellow

Working with complementary colors can be tricky. Be sure to vary shades and saturation levels.

Complementary colors of the same intensity can look like they are vibrating when placed next to each other. This can be disconcerting, to say the least.

Split Complementary Color Schemes

The color scheme uses three colors: A color and two other colors that are directly adjacent to the first color's complement on the color wheel. This provides the visual interest of a complementary color scheme but without the vibration. It also allows the use of more color. Examples include:

- Red, Yellow-Green and Blue-Green
- Yellow, Blue-Violet and Red-Violet
- Green, Red-Violet and Red-Orange

Triad Color Schemes

This color scheme makes use of three colors that are equally spaced from each other on the color wheel. Examples include:

- Red, Yellow and Blue
- Yellow, Blue-Violet and Red-Violet
- Green, Violet and Orange

Monochromatic Color Schemes

This color scheme uses two or three colors from the same color family on the color wheel. Examples include:

- Dark Blue and Light Blue
- Dark Green, Grass Green and Light Green
- Purple and Lavender

Analogous Schemes

This scheme uses one color along with the colors on either side of it on the color wheel. Examples include:

- Green, Blue-Green and Yellow-Green
- Yellow, Yellow-Green and Green
- Yellow, Yellow-Green and Yellow-Orange

Chapter 5

Vector vs Raster

Before we get into vector raster, let's seal with some basic terms.

Pixel: In Computer graphics, a pixel, dot, or picture element is a physical point in a picture. A pixel is simply the smallest addressable element of a picture represented on a screen. A majority of pictures that we see on our computer screen are raster images. The selfie that you click with your mobile phone is another example of a raster image. An image is made up using a collection of pixels referred to as a bitmap.

Bitmap: In computer graphics, a bitmap is a mapping from some domain (for example, a range of integers) to bits, that is, values which are zero or one. It is also called a bit array or bitmap index. The more general term pixmap refers to a map of pixels, where each one may store more than two colors, thus using more than one bit per pixel. Often bitmap is used for this as well. In some contexts, the term bitmap implies one bit per pixel, while pixmap is used for images with multiple bits per pixel.

Raster Graphics

Raster images use bit maps to store information. This means a large file needs a large bitmap. The larger the image, the more disk space the image file will take up. As an example, a 640 x 480 image requires information to be stored for 307,200 pixels, while a 3072 x 2048 image (from a 6.3 Megapixel digital camera) needs to store information for a whopping 6,291,456 pixels. We use algorithms that compress images to help reduce these file sizes. Image formats like jpeg and gif are common compressed image formats. Scaling down these images is easy but enlarging a bitmap makes it pixelated or simply blurred. Hence for images that need to scale to different sizes, we use vector graphics.

File extensions: .BMP, .TIF, .GIF, .JPG

Vector Graphics

Making use of sequential commands or mathematical statements or programs which place lines or shapes in a 2-D or 3-D environment is referred to as Vector Graphics. Vector graphics are best for printing since it is composed of a series of mathematical curves. As a result vector graphics print crisply even when they are enlarged. In physics: A vector is something that has a magnitude and direction. In vector graphics, the file is created and saved as a sequence of vector statements. Rather than having a bit in the file for each bit of line drawing, we use commands which describe a series of points to be connected. As a result, a much smaller file is obtained.

File extensions: SVG, EPS, PDF, AI, DXF

Conversions

1. **Vector to Raster:** Printers and display devices are raster devices. As a result, we need to convert vector images to raster format before they can be used i.e displayed or printed. The required resolution plays a vital role in determining the size of the raster file generated. Here it is important to note that the size of the vector image to be converted always remains the same. It is convenient to convert a vector file to a range of bitmap/raster file formats but going down the opposite paths is harder. (because at times we need to edit the image while converting from raster to vector)

2. **Raster to Vector:** Image tracing in computing can be referred to as vectorization and it's simply the conversion of raster images to vector images. An interesting application of vectorization is to update images and recover work. Vectorization can be used to retrieve information that we have lost. Paint in Microsoft Windows produces a bitmap output file. It is easy to notice jagged lines in Paint. In this kind of conversion, the image size reduces drastically. As a result, an exact conversion is not possible in this scenario. Due to various approximations and editing that are done in the process of conversion the converted images are not of good quality.

Chapter 6
The importance of Contracts

1. They serve as a record of commitments for both parties.

At their very core, contracts are relationships. First, two parties agree to work together and forge a connection that, if fostered well and beneficial on both sides, can last years. A contract is the visual representation of that relationship.

Contracts also hold each party to their original agreement. For example, in a SaaS contract, one party agrees to provide the other with software for a specified amount of time.

The other side agrees to pay the provider for that same amount of time. First and foremost, a contract is the trail that holds both sides accountable for the terms they set at the beginning of the relationship.

2. Agreements prevent conflicts and mitigate risk.

Contracts often go through a negotiation and redlining process that ensures both sides are getting the best deal possible. Obviously, good negotiation should lead to a mutually successful outcome that prevents conflict down the line and sets the foundation for a strong partnership moving forward.

When managed correctly, contracts should have a comprehensive audit trail of every change, comment, and edit made. Interestingly, many modern businesses have all their processes automated — with this exception.

Emails back and forth are difficult to track down and compare versions. A contract lifecycle management platform should have an online negotiation feature with a comprehensive audit trail. That way, everyone can see who made what edits at any moment in time.

3. Contracts help an entire organization maintain compliance.

Unless employees have a legal background, it's likely they're often not thinking about compliance. Luckily, having a process set in place for contracts, helps employees remember they need to create a contract that has to be approved by Legal. With modern contract management software, companies can set up contract approval workflows to make sure they stay compliant.

4. Contracts serve as a collaboration and communication tool.

From their very creation, contracts are by nature relational and collaborative. Teams can work together to determine their needs through the creation of a contract, building healthy communication, and opening up collaboration across departments.

Then, once the contract is sent out to a third party, the collaboration continues at the start of a business relationship. Next, negotiation can be used as a tool to foster a high quality of collaboration.

After a contract is signed, both sides can feel confident in the final outcome because of solid communication.

5. Ideally, agreements also help generate revenue.

Contracts are binding agreements that say one side will deliver services in exchange for payment. Furthermore, being able to have contracts processed efficiently and under the correct terms helps companies generate more revenue.

A blockade to a signed contract means a blockade to more revenue. Conversely, faster contract processes mean organizations are able to sign more deals and bring in more income.

Generating more revenue isn't just about the contract itself, but the process around it. That's why it's important to look at what tools a company uses for contracts.

Unfortunately, being stuck in the past with PDFs, email, and a stack of documents on a desk isn't going to help bring more revenue. To move to the future, the entire contract management process has to be efficient and centralized in a single source of truth.

6. Contracts increase operational efficiency.

Looking at contract management processes and evaluating the greatest needs for improvement will help organizations work more efficiently. In turn, working faster and smarter means using the right tools.

Again, a contract management platform is one of the best ways to automate contract processes. Instead of tedious emails, a few clicks means an approval is on its way. With the help of an e-signature feature, signatures take days or hours, not weeks or months.

Clearly, having all people, processes, and documents in one place is critical for aligning with the current pace of business.

7. Agreements extend a company's brand and values.

Although this may not be the first thing that comes to mind when most people think about contracts, they are an extension of the company brand. Additionally, sending out a contract is a symbol that an organization cares about having a detailed record of a relationship that they are making a commitment to.

Everything from wording to negotiations gives each party an idea of how the other functions. What's more, a solid company brand shows through care in contract creation and the interactions that follow.

The reasons to pay attention to contracts are clear. Every organization has contracts — from the first employee who is hired through every deal signed. In conclusion, ensuring processes are efficient and the tools being used are the best will help make each of these seven reasons stronger.

Tips!

- **Full scope of work to be performed, including all deliverables.**
- **General timeline or, if possible, exact due dates for each milestone.** Nothing that you discussed should be left out of the contract if you want it to be enforceable.
- **Payment amounts and terms.** How many days will the person have after delivery to remit that payment, and how will it be paid?
- **The circumstances under which the contract can be terminated and how that will be handled.** If dispute mediation becomes necessary, the contract should also outline how that will take place.
- If necessary, one or both parties may choose to include a **noncompete or nondisclosure clause.**
- **Any terms related to failed obligations.** If, for instance, payment isn't remitted by a certain date, the contract should outline what the late payment fee will apply.

If you can afford an attorney, it would be wise to have one look over your contract to make sure you've covered everything. Once you have the initial draft, you should be able to simply update it with all of your clients.

Protecting Both Parties

Let's take a look at this again, because it's so vital. Although having expectations in writing increases the odds of success, it also makes enforceability easier. Simply knowing it's in writing can put pressure on all involved parties to meet their obligations on time. The service provider will probably even routinely check the contract to make sure the work is progressing as agreed.

If an issue arises, having the agreement in writing will make enforcement much easier. If the client decides to work with a different agency halfway through the project, the provider could take legal action to be paid for work performed. On the other hand, if the service provider performs poorly, the vendor will have legal protection against paying for the work.

Locking in Financial Agreements

If written properly, your contract will make sure the service provider receives payment in a timely manner. For big projects, this generally means multiple small payments as certain milestones are reached. A publisher buying an author's book, for instance, will often issue one advance payment when the contract is signed and another when the completed manuscript is submitted.

However, a written contract may not always be enough to get paid on time. You'll still have to issue invoices in many cases and reiterate the terms on that invoice. Make it as easy as possible for your client to pay, offering as many options as possible.

Closing the Contract

Hopefully, you'll never have to take legal action based on the contract, which means the project will end and you'll move on to the next project. Both parties should keep a copy of the contract on file for several years in case a later issue should arise.

You'll also have the template that you can tweak based on the lessons you've learned from previous projects.

Chapter 7

12 Elements of Design, 7 Principles of Art, Elements of Art

I remember being in design school learning these to help me when I started my design career. This will help you gain the fundaments of design that will carry you through your design career.

Here are 12 principles of design that are commonly mentioned. Explained in the infographic below, include, balance, emphasis, contrast, proportion, hierarchy, repetition, rhythm, pattern, white space, movement, variety, and unity.

1. Balance

The balance in the design is how to arrange and position elements in the composition. It is about assigning the weight of these elements. A composition lacking in balance means that one element overpowers all the rest. To create balance, you need to position elements properly.

2. Emphasis

The purpose of emphasis is to create a focal point. A focal point is an object that stands out instantly and grabs the viewer's or user's attention at first sight. When something is emphasized in a design, it means it stands out from the rest and is significant.

It's a specific piece of content that needs to stand out from the rest of the design. When creating emphasis, make sure that it won't disturb the overall balance of the composition.

3. Contrast

Contrast is the difference between various elements whitn a design, that makes them stand out from each other. For example:The difference may be that one element has a darker background while another element has a lighter background. It is also possible that one element has a cooler tone and another has a warmer tone. Or one element is larger and the other is smaller.

4. Proportion

The proportion in the design refers to the size and visual weight of two or more visual elements. It refers to how the size of one object is compared with another and related to each other. In essence, it is the way elements are scaled relative to each other's size.

5. Hierarchy

It helps arrange the content in a logical order, from the most important to the least. Think about the typical order of elements on a web page. The most important information on a page should be at the top, so that readers will see it right away. Key information should be placed at the top of the page, where it will be most prominent and visible.

6. Repetition

Repetition means that a particular element is repeated many times throughout the design process. The role of repetition in design is to create consistency and unity. The principle often repeated in design is the logo, which plays a key role in creating brand logos.

7. Rhythm

Rhythm involves the combination of repetition, variety, and movement. Rhythm is how multiple design elements that are different from each other repeat in a particular order. Creating rhythm in design involves repeating or alternating a group of elements in the same order and at regular intervals.

8. Pattern

Patterns are nothing more than a repetition of multiple design elements working together.

Wallpaper patterns are the most common example of patterns. In design, however, patterns can also refer to set standards for how certain elements are designed. For example, top navigation is a design pattern that the majority of internet users have interacted with.

9. White space

White space is the area around existing elements that is free from visual clutter. White space refers to areas that lack of visual elements. But the areas in the design is unused white space around existing elements. White space does not mean that white space is white-It can be any color. It refers to the areas of your design where there is nothing, as well as the spaces between elements.

10. Movement

Movement is how the eyes move when viewing and interacting with a composition. Movement refers to the way the viewer's eye travels and the path it takes throughout a design. The designer uses movement to guide the viewer around different design elements.

11. Variety

Variety creates visual interest and prevents the design from becoming monotonous and predictable. Variety is created by using elements that are not similar to one another. With the use of variety, you have a good chance of maintaining the interest and engagement of viewers.

12. Unity

Design unity is that different visual elements are combined to create a cohesive, complete design with a harmonious effect. With unity, seemingly different items create a sense of 'oneness'. This can be achieved in a few different ways. Designers should understand how these design principles and elements affect their work. Looking at how other designers use these concepts can help you learn to create better designs.

The Principles of Art

Balance refers to the visual weight of the elements of the composition. It is a sense that the painting feels stable and "feels right." Imbalance causes a feeling of discomfort in the viewer.

Balance can be achieved in 3 different ways:

1. *Symmetry*, in which both sides of a composition have the same elements in the same position, as in a mirror-image, or the two sides of a face.

2. *Asymmetry*, in which the composition is balanced due to the contrast of any of the elements of art. For example, a large circle on one side of a composition might be balanced by a small square on the other side

3. *Radial symmetry*, in which elements are equally spaced around a central point, as in the spokes coming out of the hub of a bicycle tire.

Contrast is the difference between elements of art in a composition, such that each element is made stronger in relation to the other. When placed next to each other, contrasting elements command the viewer's attention. Areas of contrast are among the first places that a viewer's eye is drawn. Contrast can be achieved by juxtapositions of any of the elements of art. Negative/Positive space is an example of contrast. Complementary colors placed side by side is an example of contrast. Notan is an example of contrast.

Emphasis is when the artist creates an area of the composition that is visually dominant and commands the viewer's attention. This is often achieved by contrast.

Movement is the result of using the elements of art such that they move the viewer's eye around and within the image. A sense of movement can be created by diagonal or curvy lines, either real or implied, by edges, by the illusion of space, by repetition, by energetic mark-making.

Pattern is the uniform repetition of any of the elements of art or any combination thereof. Anything can be turned into a pattern through repetition. Some classic patterns are spirals, grids, weaves.

Rhythm is created by movement implied through the repetition of elements of art in a non-uniform but organized way. It is related to rhythm in music. Unlike pattern, which demands consistency, rhythm relies on variety.

Unity/Variety You want your painting to feel unified such that all the elements fit together comfortably. Too much unity creates monotony, too much variety creates chaos. You need both. Ideally, you want areas of interest in your composition along with places for your eye to rest.

The Elements of Art

SHAPE: A shape is a two-dimensional design encased by lines to signify its height and width.

Shapes are used to provide a symbolic and faux feeling. Shapes can have different colors to make it seem three-dimensional. There are different types of shapes like circles, triangles, and squares.

LINE: Lines are marks moving in a space between two points. Artists use many different types of lines like: Including, actual, implied, vertical, horizontal, diagonal, and contour lines. Each line has a different meaning, curve, length, thickness, and flexibility.

SPACE: Space is the distance between shapes and objects. Positive space refers to the areas of the work with a subject. Negative space is the space without a subject. Artists use spacing to create different effects.

FORM: A form is a three-dimensional object that can be held and walked around. A form can be objects like cylinders, spheres, or even hard-edged objects like cubes.

TEXTURE: Texture is usually used to describe the surface quality. Textures can be 'real' or 'implied'. Real surface quality is mainly seen through three-dimensional works, like sculptures. Implied surface quality describes how the eye perceives the texture based on visual cue.

VALUE: Value refers to the degree of perceivable lightness of tones within an image. The difference in values is called Contrast. It references the lightest and darkest tones with grey variants in between a work of art.

COLOR: Color is the spectrum of light broken down when hitting a surface and reflected into the eye. Color has various properties like 'hue' which has a basic range of colors like red and blue, 'intensity' which is the strength of a color, 'value' which is the lightness and darkness of the color, and 'temperature' which is the warmness or coolness which the viewer feels when looking at the color.

Chapter 8

Find your Flow

Finding your flow is basically finding your design style. Each graphic designers a "trademark" that sets them apart from other graphic designers.

The only way to make your work recognizable is to know what sets your designs apart. I am going to give you some actionable ways to hone in on your aesthetic so you can stand out as a designer, whether you are an illustrator, web designer, brand designer, or have another graphic design specialty.

1. Understand the brief

Understand the brief and the objectives of the project. What is the purpose, message, and tone of the design? Who is the target audience and what are their preferences? What are the deliverables, deadlines, and budget? These questions will help you define the scope and direction of your work and avoid misunderstandings and revisions later on.

2. Research and find inspiration

Research and find inspiration from other graphic designers and their work. Look for examples of similar projects, styles, and themes that match the brief and the client's brand identity. Also explore different sources of inspiration, such as art, history, nature, or trends. However, be careful not to copy or imitate other designs, but rather use them as references to create an original and unique style.

3. Experiment and refine

Elements like colors, fonts, images, and layouts can help you create different variations of your design. You can also play with different combinations, contrasts, and effects to enhance your style. Then compare and evaluate your options and select the ones that best suit the brief and the client's needs.

4. Communicate and collaborate

Communicate and collaborate with your client and other stakeholders throughout the design process. Don't be afraid to present your ideas, explain your choices, and solicit feedback. Then listen to their opinions, address their questions and issues, and incorporate their input. Doing so can build trust and rapport with your client and ensure your graphic design style aligns with their vision.

5. Learn and grow

The final step is to learn and grow from your graphic design experiences. Review your work and assess its strengths and weaknesses, challenges, and impact. Also seek feedback from your peers or mentors, and learn from their insights. Then keep track of your progress and celebrate your successes. By learning and growing continuously, you improve your skills and confidence, and develop your own graphic design voice.

As my brother said to me one day "Start where you stand.". This means to keep, going, grow and learn your craft.

Chapter 9

The Software: It's purpose

As designers we use a lot of tools to help us design and create. However, I want to focus on our computer design tools. So let's learn about Adobe Creative Cloud, which is the industry standard.

Premiere Pro

Premiere Pro is a nonlinear edited program for everything from YouTube videos to feature films. In fact, Premiere Pro has found increasing use on mainstream Hollywood films in recent years and is trending towards becoming the new industry standard editing program, though Avid Media Composer still has a strong foothold for that title as well.

Premiere Rush

Premiere Rush is a scaled down version of Premiere Pro designed specifically for on-the-go editing on a smartphone or tablet. Professional filmmakers won't find much use for Premiere Rush when Premiere Pro is at their disposal, but if you are focused on simple internet videos only, then Premiere Rush can help you reach fast turn-around times with a low barrier to entry.

After Effects

After Effects is another extremely useful program for filmmakers. After Effects is the application that you will use to handle all VFX work and any complicated digital effects.

The learning curve for After Effects is steep, but simple VFX are far more approachable with the use of After Effects than they would be otherwise.

Photoshop

Photoshop is an essential program for photographers but also finds a great deal of use from digital artists and moderate use from filmmakers. This program can be a great tool for designing a film's poster or other promotional materials and press stills. Photoshop can also be used to design art department elements to be fabricated and placed within the scene.

Acrobat DC

Acrobat DC is used for all of your PDF needs. Acrobat is essentially a document viewer that allows for enhanced interactivity with different photo and document types, especially PDFs. Useful to filmmakers for viewing and making notes or edits on a screenplay in PDF format.

Bridge

Bridge is an asset management program for centralizing files. The Adobe Bridge works in conjunction with other Adobe programs and allows for the easy transfer of files between different applications.

The Bridge can also be used to publish stock footage, to edit metadata, or to add keywords or other data to video files, making them easier to locate and organize when it comes time to edit.

Lightroom and Lightroom Classic

Lightroom and Lightroom Classic are both used for photo editing. The main difference between them is that Lightroom saves files to the cloud while Lightroom is not built for the extensive photo manipulation that can be done in Photoshop.

Instead, it is intended for more natural edits by adjusting the values of the inherent properties captured in an image.

Audition

Audition is an extensive audio editing program. It is another extremely useful program for independent filmmakers but does not find as extensive use in professional film editing as its video counterpoint: Premiere. Classic saves files to your hard drive.

Avid Pro Tools retains a firm grip over the professional audio editing market, but Audition is a viable budget-friendly alternative that will be able to get the job done on most small to mid-scale projects.

Media Encoder

Media Encoder is more of a tool than a full program. It is used to encode video files in a large variety of different formats.

Media Encoder is extremely useful for transcoding footage and for both ingesting and outputting to and from specific file types that other software programs may fail to read or process.

Mixamo

Mixamo is used in the creation, rigging, and animation of animated characters. This is a specialized animation software that won't be of any use to you as a filmmaker unless you are working in 3D animation.

Camera Raw

Camera Raw is a tool that allows the import and editing of raw photographs. This is a must-have for professional photographers, but of considerably less use to filmmakers aside from use of photography as it relates to film production.

SpeedGrade

SpeedGrade is used for color grading digital video projects. Color grading is an extremely important step in a filmmaker's editing process, and SpeedGrade offers in-depth tools and layer-based grading for crafting and fine-tuning a project's color grading.

Color can also be done in Adobe Premiere and in Adobe After Effects, but not with the same tools or level of control as in SpeedGrade. Flash Builder Premium

Flash Builder Premium is used in the building of games in the Action Script language. It likely will not be of use to a filmmaker.

Illustrator

Illustrator is the industry standard program for vector-graphics based artwork. This program may prove helpful in designing custom logos, packaging, and other design elements to appear on screen as production design elements but will be of far more use to graphic designers than filmmakers.

InDesign

InDesign is the industry standard layout and page design software. InDesign finds extensive use in the publishing industry, both for print and online, but will not be of much use to a filmmaker.

InCopy

InCopy is Adobe's proprietary word processor. The program can be used on its own or integrated directly into InDesign for publishing purposes. InCopy will not be of much use to a filmmaker.

It is not a screenwriting program, and there are plenty of other word processors for your other writing needs outside of InDesign.

XD

XD is a development program used for designing user experiences and interfaces for web and mobile. This program could be used to design a a custom user experience for the characters of a film to interact with but will otherwise not be of much use to a filmmaker.

Dimension

Dimension is primarily used for 3D brand visualizations. It can be used for product markups and packaging design previews. Dimension could be useful for a production designer on a film with a high level of custom props and set pieces but will otherwise not be of much use in filmmaking.

Aero

Aero is used to design augmented reality experiences. The program is fully launched for iOS smartphones, and the desktop versions for Windows and Mac are in public beta. This is one of the latest developments for Adobe and invites a high level of experimentation with an intuitive user experience that does not require any coding knowledge.

Aero

Aero is used to design augmented reality experiences. The program is fully launched for iOS smartphones, and the desktop versions for Windows and Mac are in public beta. This is one of the latest developments for Adobe and invites a high level of experimentation with an intuitive user experience that does not require any coding knowledge.

Animate

Animate is used, as you might guess, for animation. Adobe Animate is focused specifically on vector-based animation. 2D animation, including Flash animation, is the focus of Animate.

Filmmakers working in animation will find Animate useful, especially if their focus is on short form work with web-distribution.

Character Animator

Character Animator is used for real-time animation using facial and motion tracking. Pre-made characters are available for experimentation and facial tracking is done 100% digitally at high enough speeds to even allow for livestream animation.

The program is geared toward simplicity, speed, and ease of use, meaning it isn't ideal for complex, professional animations, but it can get the job done if you only need a quick and simple animation.

Prelude

Prelude can be accessed independently but is also integrated into Premiere Pro to assist in ingesting and logging footage. Prelude's primary function is to speed up and clean up your post-production workflow.

Chapter 10

Negative Space

Why negative space is important in design?

1. Frame Images

Negative space highlights the focal object so that the other elements of your design do not suffocate it. The effective use of negative space ensures that your viewer's eye rest on the focal point of your design.

2. Simplicity and Deception

On the whole, harnessing the power of negative space in design makes for compelling visual content that combines minimal shapes with simple iconography. This is especially useful if you want your audience to linger on your designs – in sum, it will help hold their attention for longer than just their first glance.

3. Balance Layout

Graphic design is a visual language. To allow your viewers to absorb the language of information through media and type, designers must create graphics that do not turn viewers away. Moreover, spacing elements is important so that the design is not overly complicated. Negative space brings into focus the important and subtle messages that can get lost in the elements of your design. This can happen if your design elements are overwhelmingly close together or too busy with multiple photographs or even complex color schemes.

How to use negative space?

1. Negative Space and Type

Creating meaningful visual hierarchies is essential in graphic design to make sure your viewers read the most important information first. This will be your heading or tagline, then the subheading, and then the small print. How can you achieve this? You guessed right! By inserting blank spaces between blocks of text known as negative space, you provide your viewers with legible text and readable designs.

2. Negative Spacing and Brand Logos

Do you want to start designing a visually attractive logo for your brand? Are you looking to rebrand your company logo? Wondering how negative space plays into the designing of brand logos? Simplicity is key! When designing logos, the effective use of negative space will allow for your design to remain compact, clever, and clean!

3. Negative Space and Photographs in Design

Not all designs use the elements of type, shapes, and iconography. Many effective graphics include photographs as focal points! Balancing photographs with the other elements of your design using negative space is important to make sure that the elements don't appear to crowd one another.

Overall negative space allows the eye rest as the viewer sees a design. As I said less is more. Don't clutter your design.

www.ingramcontent.com/pod-product-compliance
Lightning Source LLC
Chambersburg PA
CBHW072247170526
45158CB00003BA/1024